CASTLES AND FORTRESSES

Robert Snedden

PowerKiDS
press
New York

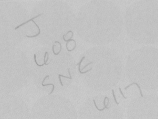

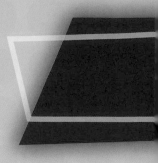

Published in 2017 by
The Rosen Publishing Group, Inc.
29 East 21st Street, New York, NY 10010

Cataloging-in-Publication Data
Names: Snedden, Robert.
Title: Castles and fortresses / Robert Snedden.
Description: New York : PowerKids Press, 2017. | Series: Engineering eurekas | Includes index.
Identifiers: ISBN 9781499430936 (pbk.) | ISBN 9781499430950 (library bound) | ISBN 9781499430943 (6 pack)
Subjects: LCSH: Castles--Juvenile literature. | Fortification--Juvenile literature.
Classification: LCC UG405.S64 2017 | DDC 623'.19--dc23

Produced for Rosen by Calcium Creative Ltd
Editors for Calcium Creative Ltd: Sarah Eason and Harriet McGregor
Designers: Paul Myerscough and Jessica Moon
Picture researcher: Rachel Blount

Picture credits: Cover: Shutterstock: Canadastock. Inside: Venetia Dean 29 artwork; Shutterstock: Aerovista Luchtfotografie 22–23, Alexander Chaikin 15r, Diak 23r, Dave Head 3, 12–13, Gail Johnson 16b, Khd 16–17, KPG Payless2 21, PHB.cz (Richard Semik) 14–15, Photology1971 13b, Eduard Pop 9b, Sergej Razvodovskij 18–19, Tudor76 5r, Supavamin Yaisoon 1, 20–21; Wikimedia Commons: 28, Saffron Blaze 6–7, Cumulus 11r, Froaringus 7t, Mediatus 8–9, Arad Mojtahedi 4–5, Myrabella 10–11, USAF photo 26–27t, 26–27b, Vigiles de Charles VII, 15th century 19r.

Manufactured in the United States of America

CPSIA Compliance Information: Batch #BW17PK: For Further Information contact Rosen Publishing, New York, New York at 1-800-237-9932.

Contents

Castle or Fortress?

Thousands of years ago, people started farming and living in one place. They realized that they must defend themselves, their crops, and their animals. One of the best ways to avoid attack by an enemy was to live somewhere that was difficult to reach and easy to defend. These places were fortresses and castles.

What is the difference between a castle and a fortress? The word fortress comes from the Latin "to make strong." **Fortifications** are buildings and constructions such as **moats** and fences that are designed to strengthen a place against attack. Many military buildings where troops and weapons are kept are known as forts. Larger forts may be called fortresses.

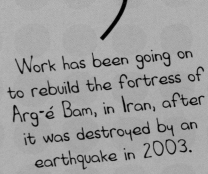

Work has been going on to rebuild the fortress of Arg-é Bam, in Iran, after it was destroyed by an earthquake in 2003.

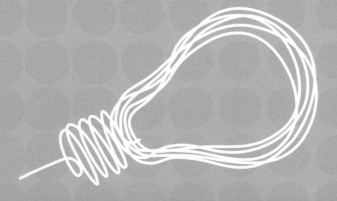

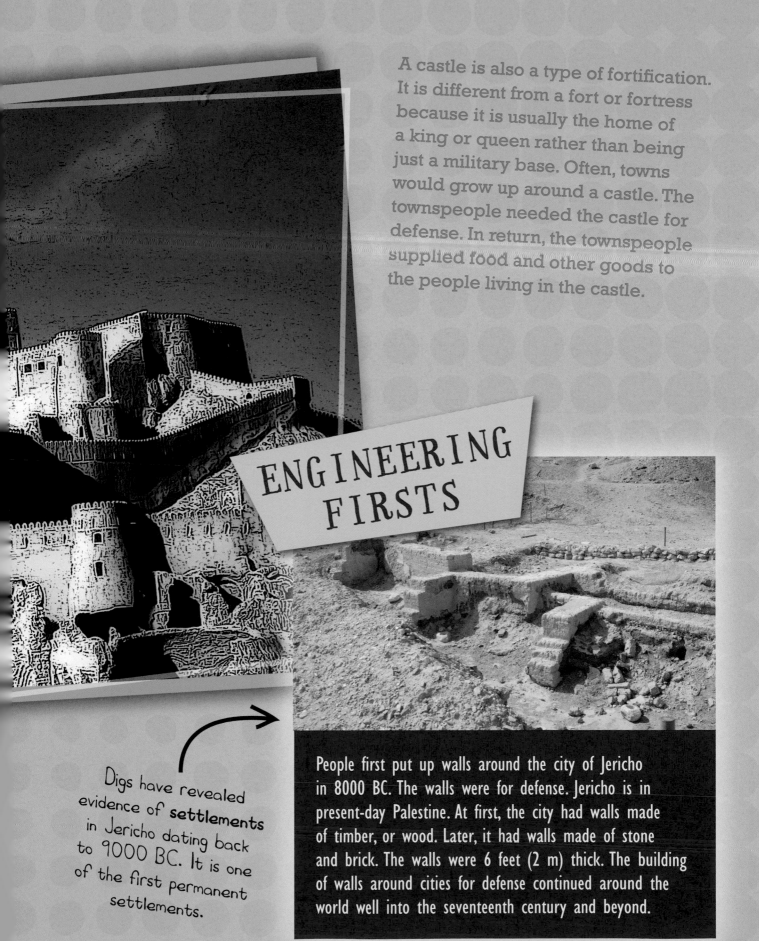

A castle is also a type of fortification. It is different from a fort or fortress because it is usually the home of a king or queen rather than being just a military base. Often, towns would grow up around a castle. The townspeople needed the castle for defense. In return, the townspeople supplied food and other goods to the people living in the castle.

ENGINEERING FIRSTS

Digs have revealed evidence of **settlements** in Jericho dating back to 9000 BC. It is one of the first permanent settlements.

People first put up walls around the city of Jericho in 8000 BC. The walls were for defense. Jericho is in present-day Palestine. At first, the city had walls made of timber, or wood. Later, it had walls made of stone and brick. The walls were 6 feet (2 m) thick. The building of walls around cities for defense continued around the world well into the seventeenth century and beyond.

First Forts

Most people in northern Europe during the Bronze and Iron Ages (2,000–4,500 years ago) lived in small villages. But some built more complicated defenses such as hill forts. Later, they built structures called **oppida**.

Hill Forts

Living on top of a hill meant you could see an enemy approaching from far away. The hill could be made harder to climb by building up banks of earth. Water-filled ditches made life even more difficult for an attacker. Where possible, natural defenses were used. For example, if one side of the hill fort was protected by high cliffs that was one less approach that needed to be defended.

Oppida

From around 200 BC, the **Celtic people** built **fortified** settlements called oppida. These were often built on high ground like hill forts, but on a much larger scale. Some oppida could hold as many as 10,000 people.

This oppidum in Spain was strengthened by stone walls and even had paved streets.

Across Europe, people began to protect their oppida by building **ramparts**. In central Europe, the ramparts were stone walls supported by banks of earth. In eastern Europe, timbers were used to support the earth ramparts. In western Europe, a timber frame was used to build the ramparts. In Britain, simple earth ramparts that were unsupported by timber were used.

The lines around this hill fort site in England show where earth ramparts were once built up.

From Oppidum to Town

Two thousand years after it was abandoned, the earth ramparts of one ancient oppidum still stand. The Titelberg, in Luxembourg in Europe, is 33 feet (10 m) high and 164 feet (50 m) wide at the base.

Oppida were used until the Romans began to conquer Europe from around 140 BC. When the Romans took control, many oppida became full Roman towns.

Roman Engineering

The Romans were the finest military engineers of the ancient world. Their military **garrison** towns were called castra. These towns were defended by ramparts and ditches. A smaller encampment was a castellum, from which the word castle comes.

This Roman gatehouse was rebuilt by historians in Germany in 1977.

The Camp

The best-known type of castrum was the camp. This was a military town in which soldiers lived. They kept their equipment and supplies there when they were not fighting or marching. Camps were usually large and rectangular. Often the buildings were made of stone. If stone was not available or there was no real threat of attack, the buildings were made of wood. A ditch dug around the outside of the camp gave extra security.

A Place for the Night

Roman army regulations required its soldiers to spend the night in a fort. If there was no permanent camp within reach, the soldiers had to build a temporary castrum. The soldiers carried with them the equipment they needed to build and stock the camp. Special engineering units directed the building of the camp. Ordinary soldiers supplied the muscle power. The Romans could construct a new camp in a few hours while under enemy attack. Construction crews first dug a trench. The material from the trench was used to build a rampart. On top of this they put a **palisade** of sharpened wooden stakes.

ENGINEERING FIRSTS

The Romans discovered how to use engineering to keep order in their camps. They always built their camps to the same plan with gates at the north, south, east, and west. Straight paths between the gates divided the camp into four. Everyone knew their place, which made the running of the camp very efficient.

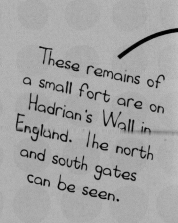

These remains of a small fort are on Hadrian's Wall in England. The north and south gates can be seen.

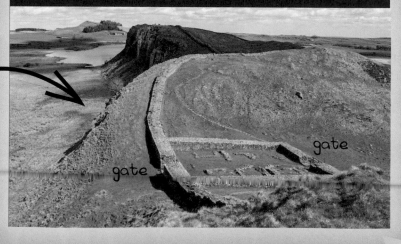

gate

gate

Motte and Bailey

After the collapse of the Roman Empire in AD 476, people began to claim land and defend it against attack. In the tenth and eleventh centuries, **motte** and **bailey** castles began to appear. These were first built in the land between the Rhine River and the Loire River in Germany and France. They then spread to the rest of western Europe.

How It Was Built

In a motte and bailey castle, the motte was a high mound of earth in the center. In the middle of the mound was a wooden tower. Around this was the palisade, a high wooden fence of pointed stakes. This was surrounded by a defensive ditch. Beyond the ditch was an outer area called the bailey, which was protected by another palisade. The motte was reached by a bridge that crossed the ditch from the bailey. This bridge could be removed if danger threatened.

The Bayeux Tapestry tells the story of the Norman invasion of England in the eleventh century. This part of it shows an attack on a motte and bailey.

No original wooden motte towers exist today. This one was rebuilt in Germany.

Location

The earliest motte and bailey castles were built wherever the ground was suitable and a good supply of timber was available. Later, they were built where they could defend trade routes, farms, and towns.

The first motte and bailey castles were built by the Normans. William of Normandy (1028–1087) conquered England in 1066. The Normans then built at least 500 mottes between 1066 and 1086. That is about one every two weeks. The mottes were built layer by layer. The first layer was made of earth, which was topped by a layer of stone, then another layer of earth, and so on. The stone layers strengthened the motte and helped with drainage. Building a motte could mean moving more than 20,000 tons (18,000 mt) of earth.

Stone Strength

The next step in castle building was to build the central tower in stone instead of wood. These stone towers were called **keeps**. They appeared in the last half of the eleventh century. One advantage to building with stone was that it made it much harder for an enemy to burn down your castle!

Keeping a Lookout

Stone keeps had thick walls and very few windows. Turrets at each corner allowed lookouts to see an enemy's approach from a long distance. The bailey was placed outside the keep but now it was surrounded by a defensive stone wall, instead of a wooden fence.

First Line of Defense

The castle's outer walls were its first line of defense. This outer wall, or **curtain wall**, surrounded the entire castle. It protected both the keep and the buildings in the bailey. The curtain walls of many castles were more than 6 feet (2 m) thick. A water-filled moat around the wall provided a further line of defense. This was crossed by a drawbridge.

The stone castle keep of Newcastle, England, was built by King Henry II (1133-1189) in 1168.

Will "fortress homes" become a feature of the future as people become more concerned about personal security? Some homes are already fitted with a "safe room." This is a fortified room that the owners can lock themselves in if their home is invaded by robbers.

Drawbridges

At its simplest, a drawbridge was a long wooden platform that was drawn back into the castle if danger threatened. Other drawbridges rotated out over the moat, a little like the way the hand of a clock moves from nine to 12. A bascule drawbridge was similar to a seesaw. It had a system of weights that pulled one side up while the other moved down. Later drawbridges were lowered on chains.

Raising the drawbridge was a great way of stopping entry to a castle.

Inside the Keep

The keep was the strongest and most heavily fortified part of a castle's defenses. If an attacker broke through the outer walls, the garrison would retreat to the keep. There they hoped to remain safe.

Bread and Beer

In the eleventh and twelfth centuries, the keep was called the *donjon*. This comes from the French word for "stronghold." Inside the stronghold was everything needed for the owner of the keep to have a comfortable life. Fancy meals for the owner and his guests were made in a kitchen. Many castles had their own bakeries to supply fresh bread for all the inhabitants. Most also had a brewery to make beer, which was run by an "ale wife."

In stone keeps, fires were lit to warm up large rooms, such as this one in Stirling Castle, in Scotland.

The Great Hall

The main area of a castle was the Great Hall. This was where most of the day-to-day activity took place. The lord of the castle would hold feasts there for important guests. He usually hoped to impress them with his wealth and power.

The Tower of London is a popular tourist destination. Nearly 3 million people visit it each year.

ENGINEERING FIRSTS

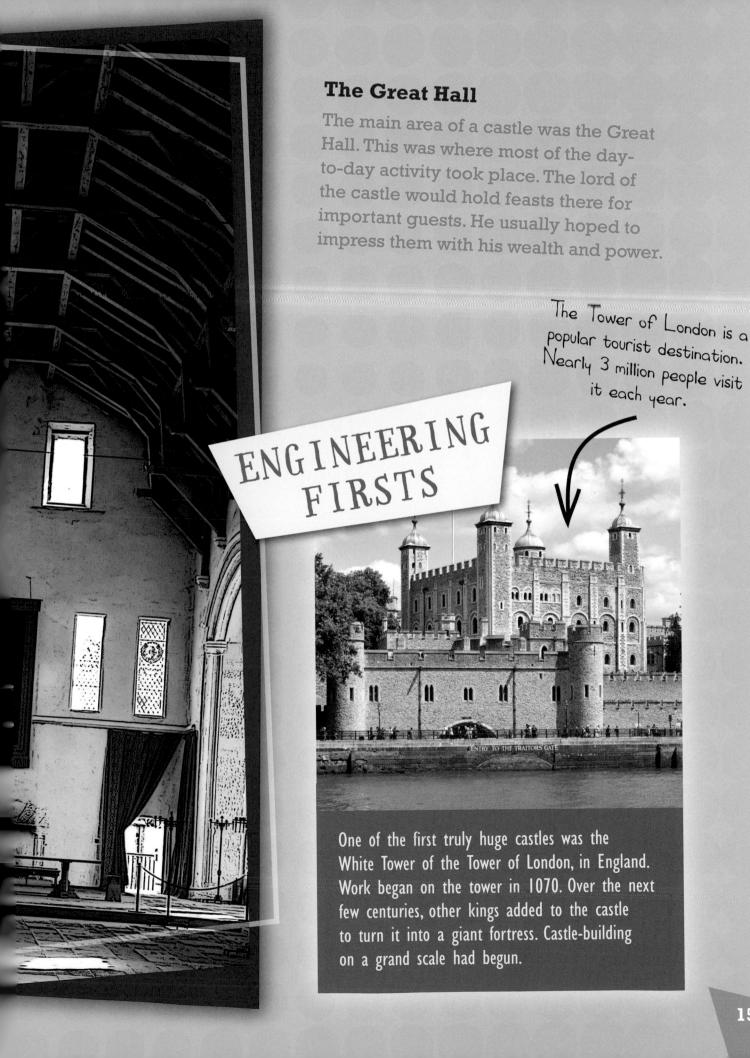

ENTRY TO THE TRAITORS GATE

One of the first truly huge castles was the White Tower of the Tower of London, in England. Work began on the tower in 1070. Over the next few centuries, other kings added to the castle to turn it into a giant fortress. Castle-building on a grand scale had begun.

Concentric Castles

A **concentric** castle is a little like two castles, one inside the other. It had two or more curtain walls, with the outer wall lower than the inner. This meant that if attackers broke through the first wall, the defenders on the inner wall could fire down on them.

ENGINEERING FIRSTS

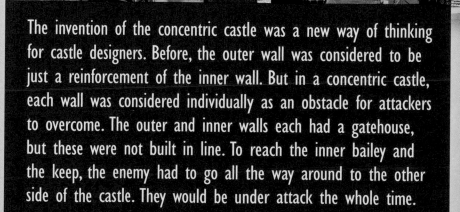

The invention of the concentric castle was a new way of thinking for castle designers. Before, the outer wall was considered to be just a reinforcement of the inner wall. But in a concentric castle, each wall was considered individually as an obstacle for attackers to overcome. The outer and inner walls each had a gatehouse, but these were not built in line. To reach the inner bailey and the keep, the enemy had to go all the way around to the other side of the castle. They would be under attack the whole time.

Work began on Beaumaris Castle, in Wales, in 1295. Its outer wall has 16 towers and two gates.

Portcullis

A **portcullis** is a gate made of wood, metal, or a combination of the two. Portcullises barred the entrances to many castles during an attack. The portcullis was mounted in vertical grooves in the castle walls. It could be quickly raised or lowered by chains or ropes attached to a winch. The winch was often in a guardroom above the gate.

An attacking army that broke through the portcullis would be caught between the inner and outer walls. There the castle's soldiers were able to fire at them from both sides.

This gatehouse with its portcullis protects entry to the medieval town of Dorat in France.

Hoardings

Wooden hoardings were often added to the inner side of the outer wall. These were like wooden roofs that reached out over the edge of the walls. They gave defenders extra protection against attack by arrows. They contained arrow loops, through which the defenders could shoot. They had holes in the floor through which things could be dropped onto any attackers below.

Capture the Castle

Military engineers were always looking for ways to beat a castle's defenses. For centuries, massive **siege towers**, battering rams, and missile-throwing devices were used against castles. In turn, the castle designers developed defenses to resist them. The battle was finally won by the invention of the cannon, which arrived in Europe by the mid-fourteenth century. The age of castle-building began to draw to an end.

The Barbican

During the later period of castle-building, an extra line of defense was added to the gatehouse. This was the barbican. It was an extension of the gatehouse and it stuck out from the castle. It was designed to be an impossible obstacle for any attackers to pass. The only way through was by a narrow, twisting path that was blocked by portcullises. **Archers** and other defenders would wait behind arrow slits and on the walls, ready to attack.

This barbican in Bulgaria is situated on a headland, giving defenders a good view of the surrounding area.

ENGINEERING FIRSTS

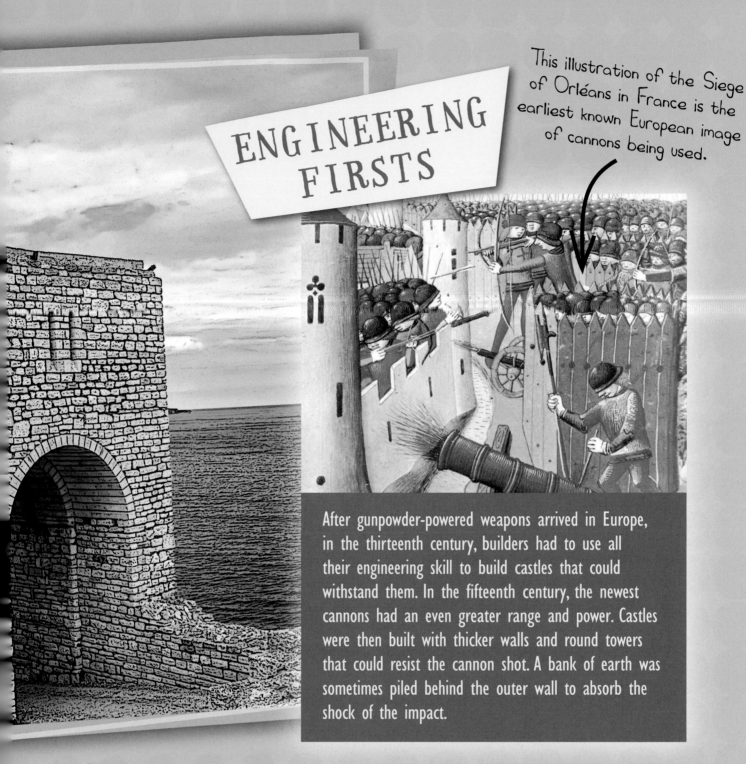

This illustration of the Siege of Orléans in France is the earliest known European image of cannons being used.

After gunpowder-powered weapons arrived in Europe, in the thirteenth century, builders had to use all their engineering skill to build castles that could withstand them. In the fifteenth century, the newest cannons had an even greater range and power. Castles were then built with thicker walls and round towers that could resist the cannon shot. A bank of earth was sometimes piled behind the outer wall to absorb the shock of the impact.

Undermining Castles

Square keeps had one weakness. Enemy miners could dig tunnels beneath the corner of the keep. They would remove the foundations (the parts below ground) and replace them with wooden props so the walls did not collapse immediately. Once enough of the stone foundations had been removed, the miners would set fire to the wooden props and escape before they burned through. Once the supports were gone, the wall collapsed.

Castles in Japan

Japanese castles used more stone in their construction than most Japanese buildings. However, they were still made mostly of wood, which means that many have been destroyed. Some also had thatched roofs made from straw, which were vulnerable to fire. Out of around 5,000 that were originally built, only 100 survive today.

Defenses

Japanese castles were located on plains, not on mountains. They relied on human-made defenses for protection and not on features of the natural environment, such as cliffs. Moats were created around the castles by diverting streams. Some castle moats were filled with water only when attack was threatened. The castle fortifications were made almost entirely of wood, with small gaps through which archers could shoot their arrows or guns could be fired.

Himeji Castle is one of the most spectacular in Japan.

Attack

Cannons were rare in Japan because the Japanese **foundries** could not easily make iron or steel cannons. Some castles had "wall guns," but these lacked the power of a true cannon. Destroying the walls of a castle was not part of the Japanese war plan. It was thought more honorable for enemy armies to fight out in the open.

Azuchi Castle was burned down in the late sixteenth century. All that is left are the stone walls.

ENGINEERING FIRSTS

Azuchi Castle was built in the 1570s, on the shores of Lake Biwa in present-day Shiga Prefecture. It was the first Japanese castle to be surrounded by high stone walls and it was built on a massive scale. It had a large stone base, with lots of concentric baileys and a tall central tower. Later castles copied the stone walls used in Azuchi Castle.

Star Forts

The star fort was first built in the mid-fifteenth century, in Italy. It came about as a response to the threat from cannon fire.

Covering Fire

In contrast to the old-style medieval castle, the star fortress was a low structure. It was made of triangular or diamond-shaped **bastions** that were designed to provide covering fire for each other. Because one bastion could defend another, it was much more difficult for enemy miners to get close and undermine the walls. A dry ditch often surrounded the fortress.

Added Defenses

Ravelins were sometimes added outside the main walls of a star fort to add further lines of defense. A ravelin was a triangular-shaped fortification placed in front of the outside wall and between the bastions. It gave the defenders yet another line of fire on their attackers. Other additions such as hornworks, two half-bastions linked by a wall, meant that the star castle could have quite a complex shape.

Fort Bourtange, in the Netherlands, was converted into a village in 1851 when it no longer had any military value.

Fort Independence in Boston, Massachusetts, was part of the harbor defenses.

ENGINEERING FIRSTS

The walls of a star fort were a new and revolutionary design. They were lower and thicker than the walls of an old-style castle. They were built using earth and brick instead of stone. This was because earth and brick do not shatter on impact from a cannonball in the way that stone does.

The Last Star Forts

The development of the explosive artillery shell in the nineteenth century meant that star forts were no longer built. Just as the cannonball had meant the end of the medieval castle a few centuries earlier, the invention of the shell had the same effect on star forts.

Global Castles

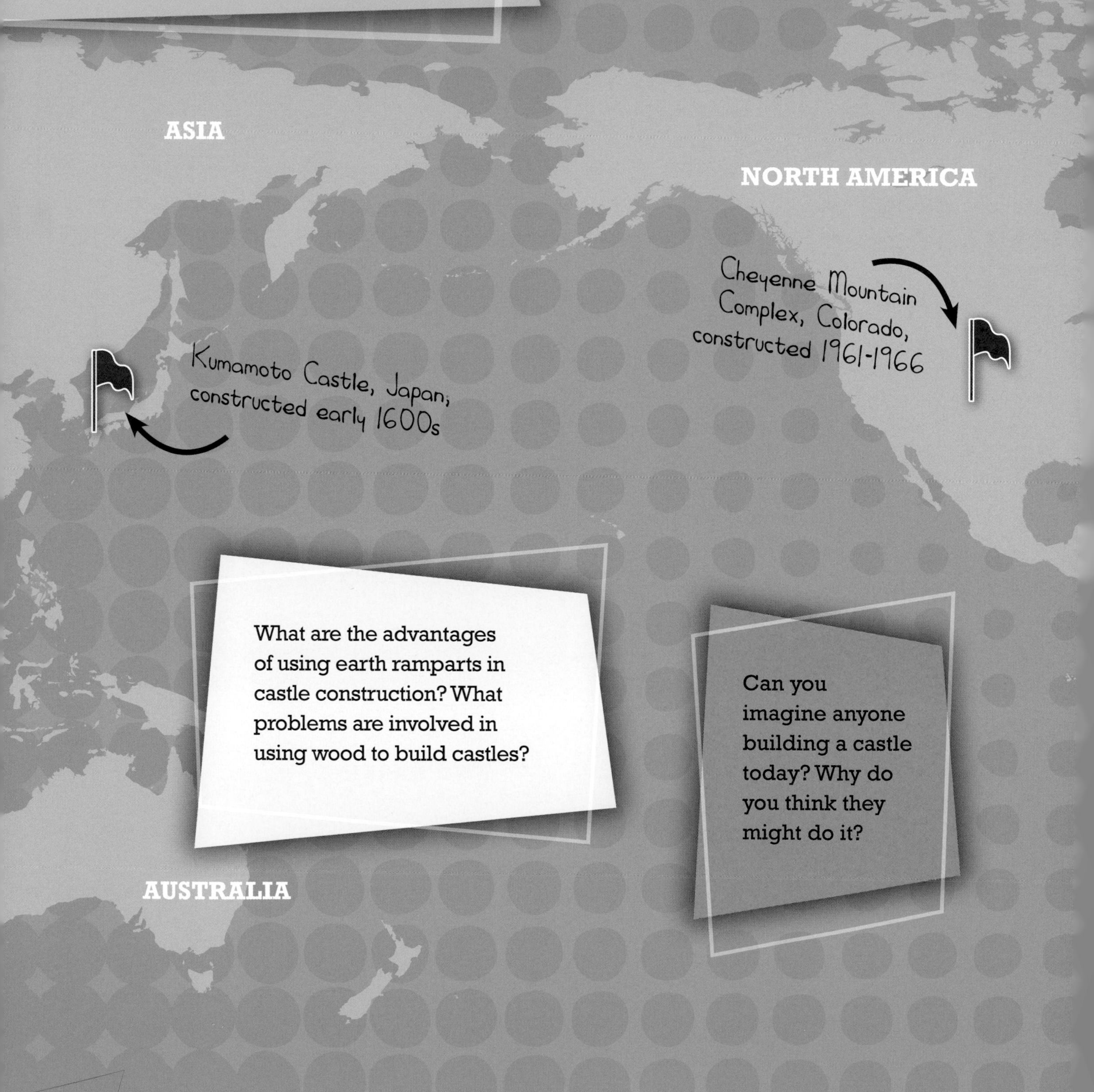

ASIA

NORTH AMERICA

Cheyenne Mountain Complex, Colorado, constructed 1961-1966

Kumamoto Castle, Japan, constructed early 1600s

What are the advantages of using earth ramparts in castle construction? What problems are involved in using wood to build castles?

Can you imagine anyone building a castle today? Why do you think they might do it?

AUSTRALIA

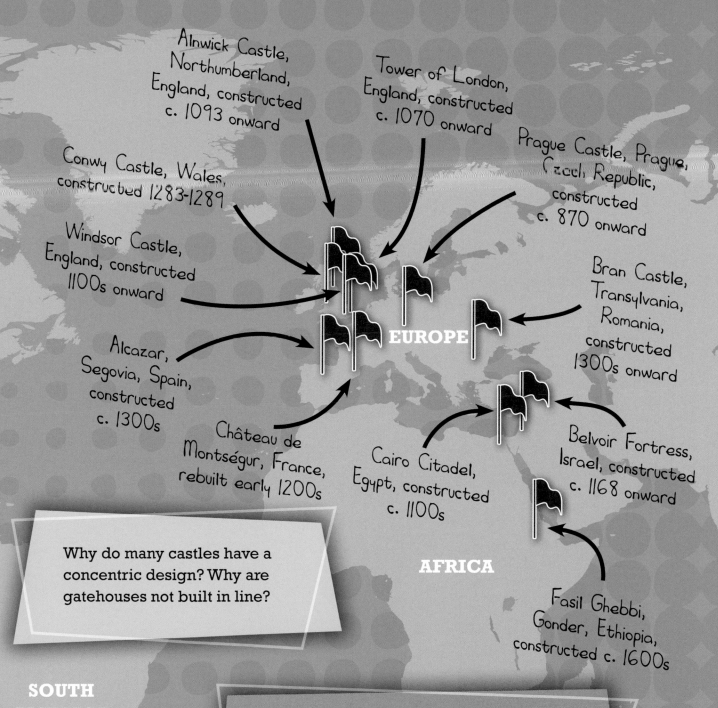

Alnwick Castle, Northumberland, England, constructed c. 1093 onward

Tower of London, England, constructed c. 1070 onward

Prague Castle, Prague, Czech Republic, constructed c. 870 onward

Conwy Castle, Wales, constructed 1283-1289

Windsor Castle, England, constructed 1100s onward

Bran Castle, Transylvania, Romania, constructed 1300s onward

Alcazar, Segovia, Spain, constructed c. 1300s

EUROPE

Château de Montségur, France, rebuilt early 1200s

Cairo Citadel, Egypt, constructed c. 1100s

Belvoir Fortress, Israel, constructed c. 1168 onward

AFRICA

Why do many castles have a concentric design? Why are gatehouses not built in line?

SOUTH AMERICA

Fasil Ghebbi, Gonder, Ethiopia, constructed c. 1600s

What part of a fortress design do you think is the most important when considering how to defend the building?

Cheyenne Mountain

At the height of the **Cold War** in the 1950s, the United States needed a command center that could withstand attack by a nuclear bomb. The result was the Cheyenne Mountain Complex. This was the ultimate fortress, built in the heart of a granite mountain.

FUTURE EUREKAS!

One forward-thinking architect firm is designing "safe houses," which are fortress-like homes. Each building has movable concrete walls that can turn the home into a big concrete cube that is impenetrable from the outside! Security codes must be keyed in by anyone wishing to enter the building.

A bus takes workers on the 1-mile (1.6 km) journey from the main entrance to the Cheyenne Mountain Complex buildings inside the mountain.

Bouncing Buildings

There are 13 three-story and 2 two-story office buildings 1 mile (1.6 km) inside the entrance to the mountain. Hallways and ramps connect the buildings. Each building is 18 inches (46 cm) away from the rock walls of the mountain to shield it from a bomb impact on the mountain. The buildings are mounted on more than 1,300 giant shock-absorbing springs. Each of these springs weighs 1,100 pounds (500 kg). The cables into the buildings that carry water and electricity are designed to flex, or bend, as the building bounces and not break.

Blast Doors

A 2-mile (3.2 km) main tunnel runs through the complex. A side tunnel leads off the main tunnel into the office buildings complex. This side tunnel is protected by two 25-ton (23 mt) blast doors. During the Cold War, one door was closed at all times. This meant that workers had to enter through the first door, then wait in a middle room for that door to close and seal behind them. They then waited for the second door to be opened so they could pass through.

Work started on the Cheyenne Mountain Complex in 1961. It took three years just to hollow out the mountain. Even now, the blast doors are closed once each day to check they work properly.

Castles of the Future?

Modern weapons mean that moats and drawbridges are no longer useful. However, wealthy people still often build their homes with tall fences and high-tech security systems to keep out intruders. Today's most fortified buildings belong to governments. They have extra-thick walls to keep their computer networks secure.

FUTURE EUREKAS!

The world's armies may not use castles anymore but they still need secure places to house people and equipment. Military engineers are always looking for new and improved forms of protection. They need blast walls to deflect the force of an exploding bomb. They have hardened hangars (buildings to house aircraft) to protect aircraft on the ground.

The headquarters of the National Security Agency at Fort Meade, Maryland, provides secure communication for the military. It is heavily fortified against cyber attack.

Why not make your own model castle using recycled paper and cardboard scraps?

You will need:
‣ A large cardboard box
‣ Scissors
‣ Glue
‣ Cardboard inner tubes from plastic wrap or toilet paper
‣ A shoe box
‣ String or thread

• Use the large cardboard box to form your castle. Cut the flaps off the box, then cut out some battlements along the walls of the castle. Keep the flaps to make a drawbridge and portcullis.
• Use cardboard tubes to make the turrets for your castle.
• Depending on the size of your outer "castle wall" box, you might want to use a shoe box to make a keep inside the castle walls. Remember to cut out a door for your castle.
• Cut the leftover flaps to size to make a gatehouse in front of the door.
• Attach your drawbridge to the gatehouse using string or thread. What else can you think of to add to your castle?

Glossary

archers People who shoot with bows and arrows.

bailey The area of a castle inside the outer wall; the outer wall is sometimes also called the bailey.

bastions Parts of a fortification that jut out from the main wall to allow defenders to fire in different directions.

Celtic people Peoples who spoke Celtic languages and lived in Europe during the Iron Age, 2,500 years ago.

Cold War A political war (1945–1990) that took place mainly between the Soviet countries and the United States.

concentric Circles or other shapes that are placed one inside the other.

curtain wall The fortified outer wall around a castle.

fortifications Defensive walls or other structures made to strengthen places against attack.

fortified Strengthened against attack.

foundries Workshops or factories where metals are cast.

garrison A group of troops stationed in a fortress.

gatehouse A fortified structure protecting the gateway to a castle or fortress.

keeps The strongest towers of castles.

moats Ditches filled with water surrounding castles or forts.

motte A mound of earth and stone that supports a tower.

oppida (singular is oppidum) Ancient Celtic fortified towns.

palisade A fence of wooden stakes fixed in the ground to form a defensive enclosure.

portcullis A strong, heavy grating of wood or metal that is lowered to block a gateway.

ramparts Defensive walls that often had a broad walkway along the top.

settlements Places where people live, such as villages, towns, or cities.

siege towers Tall towers that protected soldiers attacking a castle.

Further Reading

Books

Biesty, Stephen. *Cross-Sections Castle*. New York, NY: DK Children, 2013.

Boyer, Crispin. *Everything Castles*. Washington, DC: National Geographic Kids, 2011.

Keenan, Sheila, and David Macaulay. *Castle: How It Works*. New York, NY: Square Fish, 2015.

Weil, Ann. *The World's Most Amazing Castles*. North Mankato, MN: Raintree, 2015.

Websites

Due to the changing nature of Internet links, PowerKids Press has developed an online list of websites related to the subject of this book. This site is updated regularly. Please use this link to access the list:

www.powerkidslinks.com/ee/castles

Index